Mandarin Companion

Chinese Graded Reader

Level 1: 300 Characters

红猴的价格

Hóng Hóu de Jiàgé

The Ransom of Red Chief

by O. Henry

Mind Spark Press LLC

SHANGHAI

Published by Mind Spark Press LLC

Shanghai, China

Mandarin Companion is a trademark of Mind Spark Press LLC.

Copyright © Mind Spark Press LLC, 2017

For information about educational or bulk purchases, please contact
Mind Spark Press at business@mandarincompanion.com.

Instructor and learner resources and traditional Chinese editions of
the Mandarin Companion series are available
at www.MandarinCompanion.com.

First paperback print edition 2017

Library of Congress Cataloging-in-Publication Data
Henry, O.

The Ransom of Red Chief : Mandarin Companion Graded Readers: Level 1,
Simplified Chinese Edition / O. Henry; [edited by] John Pasden, Liu Xumei,
Chen Shishuang

1st paperback edition.

Shanghai, China / Salt Lake City, UT: Mind Spark Press LLC, 2017

Library of Congress Control Number: 2017917225
ISBN: 9781941875315 (Paperback)
ISBN: 9781941875322 (Paperback/traditional ch)
ISBN: 9781941875339 (ebook)
ISBN: 9781941875346 (ebook/traditional ch)
MCID: SFH20171208T100403

Mandarin Companion Graded Readers

Now you can read books in Chinese that are fun and help accelerate language learning. Every book in the Mandarin Companion series is carefully written to use characters, words, and grammar that a learner is likely to know.

The Mandarin Companion Leveling System has been meticulously developed through an in-depth analysis of textbooks, education programs and natural Chinese language. Every story is written in a simple style that is fun and easy to understand so you improve with each book.

Mandarin Companion Level 1

Level 1 is intended for Chinese learners at an upper-elementary level. Most learners will be able to approach this book after one to two years of formal study, depending on the learner and program. This series is designed to combine simplicity of characters with an easy-to-understand storyline which helps learners to expand their vocabularies and language comprehension abilities. The more they read, the better they will become at reading and grasping the Chinese language.

Level 1 is based on a core set of 300 fundamental characters, ensuring each book's vocabulary will be simple everyday words that the reader is most likely to know. Level 1 books contain approximately 400 unique words, introducing a limited number of new key words relevant to the story.

Key words are added gradually over the course of the story accompanied by a numbered footnote for each instance. Pinyin and an English definition are provided at the bottom of the page for the first instance of each key word, and a complete glossary is provided at the back of the book. All proper nouns have been underlined to help the reader distinguish between names and other words.

What level is right for me?

If you are able to comfortably read this book without looking up lots of words, then this book is likely at your level. It is ideal to have at most only one unknown word or character for every 40-50 words or characters that are read.

Once you are able to read fluidly and quickly without interruption you are ready for the next level. Even if you are able to understand all of the words in the book, we recommend that readers build fluency and reading speed before moving to higher levels.

How will this help my Chinese?

Reading extensively in a language you are learning is one of the most effective ways to build fluency. However, the key is to read at a high level of comprehension. Reading at the appropriate level in Chinese will increase your speed of character recognition, help you to acquire vocabulary faster, teach you to naturally learn grammar, and train your brain to think in Chinese. It also makes learning Chinese more fun and enjoyable. You will experience the sense of accomplishment and confidence that only comes from reading entire books in Chinese.

Extensive Reading

After years of studying Chinese, many people ask, "why can't I become fluent in Chinese?" Fluency can only happen when the language enters our "comfort zone." This comfort comes after significant exposure to and experience with the language. The more times you meet a word, phrase, or grammar point the more readily it will enter your comfort zone.

In the world of language research, experts agree that learners can acquire new vocabulary through reading only if the overall text can be understood. Decades of research indicate that if we know approximately 98% of the words in a book, we can comfortably "pick up" the 2% that is unfamiliar. Reading at this 98% comprehension level is referred to as "extensive reading."

Research in extensive reading has shown that it accelerates vocabulary learning and helps the learner to naturally understand grammar. Perhaps most importantly, it trains the brain to automatically recognize familiar language, thereby freeing up mental energy to focus on meaning and ideas. As they build reading speed and fluency, learners will move from reading "word by word" to processing "chunks of language." A defining feature is that it's less painful than the "intensive reading" commonly used in textbooks. In fact, extensive reading can be downright fun.

Graded Readers

Graded readers are the best books for learners to "extensively" read. Research has taught us that learners need to "encounter" a word 10-30 times before truly learning it, and often many more times for particularly complicated or abstract words. Graded readers are appropriate for learners because the language is controlled and simplified, as opposed to the language in native texts, which is inevitably difficult and often demotivating. Reading extensively with graded readers allows learners to bring together all of the language they have studied and absorb how the words naturally work together.

To become fluent, learners must not only understand the meaning of a word, but also understand its nuances, how to use it in conversation, how to pair it with other words, where it fits into natural word order, and how it is used in grammar structures. No textbook could ever be written to teach all of this explicitly. When used properly, a textbook introduces the language and provides the basic meanings, while graded readers consolidate, strengthen, and deepen understanding.

Without graded readers, learners would have to study dictionaries, textbooks, sample dialogs, and simple conversations until they have randomly encountered enough Chinese for it to enter their comfort zones. With proper use of graded readers, learners can tackle this issue and develop greater fluency now, at their current levels, instead of waiting until some period in the distant future. With a stronger foundation and greater confidence at their current levels, learners are encouraged and motivated to continue their Chinese studies to even greater heights. Plus, they'll quickly learn that reading Chinese is fun!

About Mandarin Companion

Mandarin Companion was started by Jared Turner and John Pasden who met one fateful day on a bus in Shanghai when the only remaining seat left them sitting next to each other. A year later, Jared had greatly improved his Chinese using extensive reading but was frustrated at the lack of suitable reading materials. He approached John with the prospect of creating their own series. Having worked in Chinese education for nearly a decade, John was intrigued with the idea and thus began the Mandarin Companion series.

John majored in Japanese in college, but started learning Mandarin and later moved to China where his learning accelerated. After developing language proficiency, he was admitted into an all-Chinese masters program in applied linguistics at East China Normal University in Shanghai. Throughout his learning process, John developed an open mind to different learning styles and a tendency to challenge conventional wisdom in the field of teaching Chinese. He has since worked at ChinesePod as academic director and host, and opened his own consultancy, AllSet Learning, in Shanghai to help individuals acquire Chinese language proficiency. He lives in Shanghai with his wife and children.

After graduate school and with no Chinese language skills, Jared decided to move to China with his young family in search of career opportunities. Later while working on an investment project, Jared learned about extensive reading and decided that if it was as effective as it claimed to be, it could help him learn Chinese. In three months, he read 10 Chinese graded readers and his language ability quickly improved from speaking words and phrases to a conversational level. Jared has an MBA from Purdue University and a bachelor in Economics from the University of Utah. He lives in Shanghai with his wife and children.

Credits

Original Author: O. Henry

Editor-in-Chief: John Pasden

Content Editor: Chen Shishuang

Adapted by: Liu Xumei

Illustrator: Hu Sheng

Producer: Jared Turner

Acknowledgments

We are grateful to Liu Xumei, Chen Shishuang, Tan Rong, and the entire team at AllSet Learning for working on this project and contributing the perfect mix of talent to produce this series.

Thank you also to our awesome testers, Kendra Lindsay, Vanessa Dewey, and Janee Bethea.

Finally, thanks to *Journey to the West* for providing just the right cultural context to allow us to adapt this classic short story to a Chinese context.

Table of Contents

Story Adaptation Notes

Perhaps best known for *The Gift of the Magi*, O. Henry is a well-known American writer of short stories. Written in 1910, the story *The Ransom of Red Chief* brilliantly tapped into a rich vein of comedy associated with the many difficulties of caring for a mischievous child. The "Red Chief" in the title, however, calls attention to the very different culture of the time, when "cowboys and Indians" was the most common game all children knew, and the United States had barely even begun to address its real issues of racial equality.

This Mandarin Companion graded reader has been adapted into a fully localized Chinese version of the original story. Alabama around the turn of the century is swapped out for backwoods Shanxi around the turn of the millennium. The characters have been given authentic Chinese names as opposed to transliterations of English names, which sound foreign in Chinese.

Clearly, the original "Red Chief" does not work in a Chinese context, even though the story's larger theme of a child so unruly that he can barely be contained is all too familiar in the modern Chinese one-child household. And yet Chinese kids do have a uniquely Chinese hero all their own, unparalleled in his naughtiness: Sun Wukong, the Monkey King from *Journey to the West*. Thus, our story uses its own version of Sun Wukong, a modern-day, fictional caped simian superhero named 红猴 (Hóng Hóu), and gleefully jettisons the anachronistic "Red Chief." You won't miss him at all.

Character Adaptations

The following is a list of the characters from *The Ransom of Red Chief* in Chinese followed by their corresponding English names from Henry's original story. There are, of course, other characters in the story besides these, but many do not have exact correspondences to the original. The names below aren't translations; they're new Chinese names used for the Chinese versions of the original characters. Think of them as all-new characters in a Chinese story.

老马 (Lǎo Mǎ) - Bill

林哥 (Lín Gē) - Sam

高先生 (Gāo Xiānsheng) - Dorset

红猴 (Hóng Hóu) - Johnny

Cast of Characters

老马
(Lǎo Mǎ)

林哥
(Lín Gē)

高先生
(Gāo Xiānsheng)

红猴
(Hóng Hóu)

Locations

西安 (Xī'ān)

The capital of Shaanxi Province, Xi'an is famous for being one of the Four Great Ancient Capitals and home of the famous Terracotta Warriors. In this story Xi'an is simply the largest city in this area of China's relatively less prosperous northwest region.

山西 (Shānxī)

Not to be confused with next-door province "Shaanxi" (where Xi'an is), Shanxi Province in northern China is arid and mountainous.

Chapter 1
一个生意

1995 年的一天，我和老马 来到了山西的一个村子。那时候，我们很想去西安 做生意，可是只有六百多块钱。

"不行，"我对老马 说，"六百多块太少了。我们要买 吃的东西，还要坐车。如果去西安 做生意，最少还要两千块。"

"可是我们去哪儿找那么多钱?"老马看起来 很不开心。

"我们可以先在这里做一个小'生意'。"我看着前面的村子 说。

---

1 村子 (cūnzi) *n.* village, town
2 生意 (shēngyì) *n.* business
3 买 (mǎi) *v.* to buy
4 起来 (qǐlai) *v.* to get up
5 开心 (kāixīn) *adj.* happy

这个村子 不太大，人也不多，但是每家都很有钱。大人们去工作的时候，孩子们就在一起玩。他们开心 的笑 声让我想到了一个好办法。

"村子 里的人很爱他们的孩子，他们也很有钱。如果我们抓 走一个孩子，他的父母一定会给我们钱，让我们放 孩子回家。这里没有警察，别的村子 的警察 来的时候，我们早就跑 了。"

"这个办法 好。"老马 开心 地说，"村子西边有一个山，山上有个山洞，我们可以买 一些吃的放 在那里。抓 到孩子以后，就带 他去那儿。"

---

6 有钱 (yǒuqián) *adj.* rich; to have money
7 笑 (xiào) *v.* to laugh, to smile
8 想到 (xiǎngdào) *vc.* to think of
9 办法 (bànfǎ) *n.* way of doing
10 抓 (zhuā) *v.* to grab
11 放 (fàng) *v.* to put, to release
12 警察 (jǐngchá) *n.* police
13 跑 (pǎo) *v.* to run
14 山洞 (shāndòng) *n.* cave (in the mountains)
15 带 (dài) *v.* to carry

我们都觉得抓 高先生 的儿子最好。

高先生 是村子 里最有钱 的人，两千块这

个价格 对他来说，应该不高。再说，他只

有一个八岁的儿子，所以他一定会给钱的。

我和老马 在他家外面看了几天，高先生

不在家的时候，孩子就在外面玩。他只有八岁，但是力气 不小，常常打别的孩子。村子 里的孩子都不喜欢跟他一起玩，所以他总是一个人玩。

村子 里的大人也不喜欢这个孩子，因为他常常拿 别人家的东西，还用石头 在别人的车上写字。他一直以为 别人都不知道是他做的坏事。别人问他的时候，他也从来不 说"对不起"。

高先生 的儿子不喜欢上学。如果高先生 发现 儿子没去上学，一定会打他。可是，他儿子还是 不听话，高先生 也没办法。

17 力气 (lìqi) *n.* strength
18 拿 (ná) *v.* to pick up
19 石头 (shítou) *n.* stone
20 以为 (yǐwéi) *v.* to (mistakenly) think that
21 从来不 (cónglái bù) *phrase* never

22 上学 (shàngxué) *vo.* to go to school
23 发现 (fāxiàn) *v.* to discover
24 还是 (háishi) *conj.; adv.* still; had better
25 听话 (tīnghuà) *vo.* to be obedient, to listen

"这个孩子是不好管，"老马 说，"不过，
如果我是他爸爸，我一定会想办法 让他
听话。"

"对，他只是一个八岁的孩子，我们是

大人，一定有办法 管 他。"我想了一下，又

说："明天等 高先生 出门，我们就去抓 人，

然后给高先生 写信 要钱。"

"林哥，我们很快 就有钱 去西安 做

生意 了！"老马 开心 地笑 了，"明天我们先

去买 一些吃的放 在山洞 里，再去抓 人。"

27 等 (děng) *v.* to wait

28 出门 (chūmén) *vo.* to go out the door

29 信 (xìn) *n.* letter

30 很快 (hěn kuài) *phrase* quickly, soon

Chapter 2
抓人

第二天早上，我和老马 开车 去买 了一些孩子喜欢吃的东西。

"孩子都爱吃这些东西，如果给他吃这个，他一定会跟我们走的。"买 好东西以后，我开心 地说。

"对，如果孩子高兴，这件 事就会很好办。"老马 也笑 了，"如果孩子一直大哭大叫，别人一定会发现 我们。"

十点多的时候，我们开车 到了高先生家外面，他已经出门 了。他儿子一个人坐

---

31 开车 (kāichē) *vo.* to drive (a car)
32 高兴 (gāoxìng) *adj.* happy
33 件 (jiàn) *mw.* [measure word for clothing, incidents]

34 哭 (kū) *v.* to cry
35 大叫 (dàjiào) *v.* to cry out loudly

在门口玩石头。

"小孩儿，要不要吃这个？很好吃的。"
老马 一边问，一边拿 出好吃的。

孩子看了我们一下，没有说话，又去
玩石头。

我又问了一次，孩子还是 不说话。
老马 看孩子一直不说话，很不高兴，大声
问："小孩儿，听不见我们的话吗？！"

老马 刚说完，孩子手里的石头 就打
到了他头上。

"啊……"老马 大叫 了一声，"我的头！
你用石头 打我！林哥，我要让高先生 多给
五百块！"

"老马，小声点。我们的价格 可以高

36 大声 (dàshēng) *adv.* loudly

一点，这个晚上再说。"我小声说。

"可是吃的东西对他没有用，怎么办？"

老马 说。

"我有办法。"我走过去，笑 着对孩子

说："小孩儿，我们的车很大，你想不想和

我们一起坐车去山里玩？我们在山里放了很多好吃的东西。"

"真的吗？你们要带我去山里玩？还能坐车？"孩子高兴地叫了起来，"太好了，我一直想去山里玩！"

"那我们快点上车吧。"我一边说，一边让老马打开车门。

路上，老马对孩子说："我是大人，孩子不可以打大人。以后你再打我，我就打你，听见了吗？"

孩子看了看老马："如果你打我，我就让我的朋友红猴来打死你。"

"你的朋友？他在哪儿呢？"老马笑了起来。"我是大人，怎么会怕两个孩子？"

---

37 打开 (dǎkāi) vc. to open　　　38 怕 (pà) v. to fear

老马 刚说完，孩子就用力打了一下他的头："等 红猴 明天来了，一定会让你知道他的厉害。"

"啊……你这个小孩儿！"老马大叫。"林哥，这个孩子的力气 真大！"

"老马，别说了！"说完，我又对孩子说："小孩儿，你要听话，别再打老马 了。一会儿我们给你好吃的。"

回到山洞 以后，我让老马 去拿 一些吃的，孩子跟我们一起坐在地上，吃得很开心。

"山里真好，我真喜欢这里！"孩子一边吃一边说。"我爸爸总是管 我，不让我来山里玩。这些东西真好吃，比我家的饭

---

39 用力 (yònglì) vo. to use force   40 厉害 (lìhai) adj. impressive

好吃多了！"孩子说完，又吃了一大口。"这

个山洞 怎么这么大？我们晚上睡在哪儿？
　　14

老马，再给我拿 点儿吃的。你们知道我的
　　　　　18

朋友红猴 吗？老马，等 明天红猴 来了，你
　　27

就会知道他有多厉害……"
　　　40

"小孩儿，你想不想爸爸？想不想回家？"我问孩子。

"回家多没意思，我才不想回家呢！我喜欢在这里跟你们一起玩。"孩子高兴地说。

"好啊，那你就在这里跟我们一起玩几天再回家吧。"我笑着说。我很高兴孩子这么喜欢这里，这样他就会好好在这里玩，不会很难管的。老马也可以放心地跟他一起玩了。

晚上睡觉以前，老马在地上放了几件很大的衣服，睡在上面一点也不冷。

我和老马都累坏了，很快就睡着了。

---

41 放心 (fàngxīn) *v.* to relax
42 睡觉 (shuìjiào) *vo.* to sleep
43 衣服 (yīfu) *n.* clothing
44 累 (lèi) *adj.* tired
45 睡着 (shuìzháo) *vc.* to fall asleep

— Chapter 3 —
红猴来了

"坏人，你们怕 我吗?"早上六点，我
和老马 还在睡觉，就听见有人在大叫。

"林哥，会不会是村子 里的人来抓 我
们了?"老马 很快 穿 上衣服，小心 地走到
洞口，看了一会儿，说:"奇怪！一个人都
没有。"

"坏人就是你们 !"是孩子在说话。

"林哥 !"老马 大叫 了一声,"是孩子 !
他在树 上……"

我也很快 就起来 了，穿 衣服 的时候，

---

46 穿 (chuān) *v.* to put on, to wear　　49 奇怪 (qíguài) *adj.* strange
47 小心 (xiǎoxīn) *v.* to be careful　　50 树 (shù) *n.* tree
48 洞口 (dòngkǒu) *n.* mouth of a cave

我发现 衣服 后面写着两个大字"坏人"。

"一定是孩子写的！"我一边想，一边往 外走。老马 的衣服 上也写了这两个字，不过他好像 没发现。

山洞 前面有一个大树，孩子很开心 地坐在上面。不过，他换 了一件 红衣服，现在看起来 有点像 猴子。

"小孩儿，你穿 的是什么衣服？"我笑着问。

"我是红猴！不要叫我小孩儿！"孩子大声 说，"你们都小心 点，红猴 很厉害的！"

"好吧，"我说，"我们叫你红猴。红猴，听话，下来！"

---

51 往 (wǎng) *cov.* toward
52 好像 (hǎoxiàng) *adv.* it seems (that)
53 换 (huàn) *v.* to change
54 像 (xiàng) *v.* to resemble

"我不下去，红猴 就喜欢在树 上。"

"小孩儿，快下来，听见没有？！"老马

对红猴 大叫，"如果你不听话，我就让你哭

着回家找爸爸！"

很快，红猴就从树上下来了，他生气地对老马说："我再说一次，我是红猴！不要叫我小孩儿！你总是要管我，你是不是觉得自己很厉害？"红猴想了一下，从地上拿起了一只虫子，又说："如果你真的那么厉害，那就吃了这个虫子吧！"

"啊……不要啊！"老马大叫，"红猴，你厉害，你最厉害……"

红猴觉得这样很好玩，一下子骑到了老马身上。他拿出吃饭用的刀，大声说："再说一次，红猴比我厉害！快说！"

"林哥，快抓住他！他有刀！他真的会杀死我的！"老马怕死了，大叫起来。

---

55 生气 (shēngqì) vo. to get angry
56 虫子 (chóngzi) n. bug, insect, worm
57 好玩 (hǎowán) adj. fun, amusing
58 一下子 (yīxiàzi) adv. all at once
59 骑 (qí) v. to ride on
60 身上 (shēnshang) n. on one's body
61 抓住 (zhuāzhù) vc. to grab hold of

我用力 拿 走红猴 手里的刀："好了好
了，红猴，别打了！老马 只是说说，我们
不会真的送 你回家的。"

红猴 坐在地上，看起来 也有点累 了。

62 送 (sòng) *v.* to send, to deliver, to
take (someone to a place)

我让老马 去给他拿 吃的，红猴 吃得很快。

"红猴，你这么早起来，昨天一定没睡好吧？"我小心 地问，"吃好以后去换 一件衣服，再睡一会儿，好不好？"

"我吃好了，我现在就想睡。"说完，他就换 上了昨天的衣服，红衣服 就放 在地上。

孩子睡着 以后，老马 小声说："林哥，快点拿 走他的衣服。没有这件 衣服，红猴就不会来了。"

"这件 衣服 你放 到山洞 外面去，这样他就找不到了。"我对老马 说。

"林哥，我还是 不放心。我们快点给高先生 写信 要钱吧。这个孩子太厉害 了！

他那么喜欢玩刀，我怕 他真的会杀死我。"

老马 听起来 很怕 这个孩子。

"你说得对，我们今天就写信。"

Chapter 4
写信

"林哥，你是不是也怕 红猴？"老马 看看我，小声地问。

"怕 什么？ 他只是一个八岁的孩子。"

老马 看了一下孩子，问："你觉得高先生 会给我们钱吗？ 他儿子那么厉害……"

"放心 吧，他一定会给的。这个孩子是很难管，可是他只有这一个儿子。"

不知道是不是我们说话太大声 了，孩子很快 就起来 了："我的衣服 呢？你放 在哪儿了？"孩子抓 着老马 问。

"我也不知道。"老马 笑 着说。

"我不相信！我要去找我的衣服。"孩
子说完就往外走。

"老马，我们现在就写信。"我小声
说，"我们要快点拿到两千块，去西安做

63 相信 (xiāngxìn) v. to believe

生意。听说西安 有很多好吃的东西，好玩
的地方。"

"不行！"老马 看着我，"两千块不行！
这个孩子打了我那么多次，我一定要多拿
五百块！不！一千块！"

"你说得对，那我们的价格 就是三千
块！"想到 能多拿 一千块，我也很开心。
很快 我就写好了给高先生 的信。

高先生：

你好！不要问我们是谁，你儿子在
我们这儿！给我们三千块钱，我们
就会让你的儿子回家！在村子 的
西面有一个山，山下有一个很高
的树，树 的下面有一块石头。今
天下午五点半，你让人放 三千块

钱在下面。我们拿 到钱以后，就
会让你儿子回家。你不给钱，就
见不到你儿子！如果我们发现 你
告诉 了警察，你也别想再见到你
儿子了！

两个不怕 死的人

"老马，我十点就去送 信。这样的话，
高先生 今天就能看到信 了。"

"好，太好了！"老马 高兴 地说。

"你们两个在说什么？"孩子走了进来，
手里还拿 着红猴 的衣服！

"你是怎么找到衣服 的？"我和老马 都
没想到 他这么快就找到了红猴 的衣服。

---

64 告诉 (gàosu) *v.* to tell

65 没想到 (méi xiǎngdào) *phrase* to never have imagined

"衣服 就在树 上，很好找，我一下子
就看到了。"孩子很开心，拿 起衣服 想要
穿。

"林哥，我以为 衣服 放 在树 上，他一
定找不到。没想到 他还是 找到了。"老马
看着我，快要哭 了。

"如果孩子换 上红猴 的衣服，就……"
想到 这儿，我问孩子："对了，我们还有很
多好吃的。如果你想吃，我们现在就做饭
给你吃，好不好？"

"什么好吃的？"孩子马上 放下 衣服，
跑 了过来。

"做饭很好玩 的，你坐在这里看我们
做吧？"看见孩子没穿 红猴 的衣服，我就

---

66 马上 (mǎshàng) *adv.* right away   67 放下 (fàngxia) *vc.* to put down

放心了。

"你去做饭，让老马来跟我玩。"孩子开心地说。

老马看看我，说："还是我来做饭吧，我做饭很好吃的。"

"不行，我就要你跟我玩。"孩子刚说完，就从地上拿起一只很大的虫子，放进了老马的衣服里。

"啊……虫子！"老马大叫。

"太好玩了！太好玩了！"孩子一边笑一边跑。

"别跑！你这孩子，我今天一定要打你！"老马很生气，跑过来要打孩子。

"你打我，我就让红猴打你们！"孩子

大声 说。
36

　　"小孩儿，我们昨天不是说好了吗？
你要听话，不能打老马。"我笑 着对孩子
25　　　　　　　　　　　　　7
说。"我和老马 给你做好吃的，还跟你一起
玩，还有谁会对你这么好？"

"好，我不打他。但是，过一会儿你要让他跟我玩骑马。"孩子说。

"没问题。那你先自己去外面玩，我们给你做好吃的。"我说。

我知道老马很怕跟孩子一起玩，可是我也没有办法。我现在只想快点给高先生送信，拿到钱以后快点去西安。

Chapter 5
送信

"林哥，你真的要让我一个人跟他玩？"

"我知道这孩子有点可怕，跟他一起玩很累。"我一边做饭一边说。"可是，我们一定要有一个人在这里。如果孩子不见了，我们就拿不到钱了。"

老马还是不高兴，可是他也没有更好的办法。

我看老马不说话，又说："别怕，他只是个八岁的孩子，不要让他穿上红猴的衣服就好。我很快就回来。"

做好饭以后，老马去叫孩子来吃。十

点左右，我就开车 下山去送 信 了。

进村子 的时候，我看见一个老人坐在树 下。

"你好，我要送 信 给村子 里的一个人。如果现在送，他下午能拿 到信 吗?"我问。

"放心 吧，一定能。"

"太好了！今天晚上我们就能拿 到钱了。"我开心 地想。

信 送 出去以后，时间还早，所以我没有马上 回去。我在村子 里一边走，一边想:"孩子一天没回家，不知道高先生 他们家人是不是都在找他。"走到高先生 家大门外的时候，一个女人从里面 走了出来。我想了一下，笑 着走了过去。

69 里面 (lǐmiàn) *n.* inside

"你好，我想买 肉 包子，你知道哪儿
　　　　　　3　70　　71

有卖 的吗？"
　72

　　"你是外地来的吧？"她也笑 了，"前面
　　　　　　　　　　　　　　　7

就有一个包子 店，我带 你一起去吧，我也
　　　　　71　　　　15

---

70 肉 (ròu) *n.* meat 　　　　72 卖 (mài) *v.* to sell
71 包子 (bāozi) *n.* steamed bun

要买 肉 包子。"

"谢谢你。对了，你认识高先生 吗？"

"当然，我就在他家工作。"她看了我一下，又说："他是我们村子 里最有钱 的人，谁都知道他。"

"听说高先生 只有一个儿子，他一定很爱这个孩子吧。"我这么说是因为拿 到钱以后，我就不会再来这个村子 了，所以我不怕 有人知道我来过这里。

听了我的话，女人笑 了一下，又说："这个孩子很爱玩，很难管，高先生 也没办法管 他。对了，他儿子这两天不见了。"

"不见了？ 那高先生 一定在找他吧？"我问。

"不用 找，这孩子应该很快 就会回来的。"女人说。

"不会吧？如果是坏人抓 走的怎么办？高先生 一点儿都不怕？"

"这孩子常常一个人跑 出去玩，他不会有事的。"女人笑 着说。

我不知道女人为什么会这么说。不过，高先生 只有这一个儿子，一定不会不管他，所以我相信 他还是 会给钱的。

买 好包子 以后，我就回去了。还没走到洞口，就听到红猴 大声 说："别说话了！你是马，马是不会说话的。"

"不要拿 这个打我的头 !"老马大叫，"你再打我，我就不跟你玩了 !"

---

73 不用 (bùyòng) *phrase* no need

"马都爱吃草，地上有那么多草，你怎么不吃？快吃啊！"

"我是人，不是真的马……"老马 好像哭了。

"那你为什么叫老马？你叫老马，就应该像 马一样吃草。"红猴 笑 着说。

我走进去一看，红猴 骑 在老马 的身上，开心 地叫："跑 快点，跑 快点！"他一边骑 一边打老马 的头。

"红猴，快下来！我有话要跟老马 说。"

"林哥，你怎么才回来？"老马 听起来快没力气 了。

"你去哪儿了？"红猴 跑 过来问我。"你手里拿 的是什么？"

---

74 草 (cǎo) *n.* grass

"我买 了好吃的。你先出去玩一会儿，
过一会儿我们一起吃。"

红猴 出去以后，老马 还坐在地上。他

身上 的衣服 有点破 了，看起来 累 坏了。

"林哥，你知道我今天是怎么过的吗?

---

75 破 (pò) *adj.* worn out, beat-up

这孩子力气 太大了，我快累 死了……你
看我的衣服，这里都破 了。"

"我们很快 就有钱 了，等 我们拿 到
钱，就给你买 新衣服。"

"信 送 好了吗?"老马 问。

"送 好了，高先生 下午就能看到信。
我们今天一定能拿 到钱。"

"太好了！我们拿 到钱就送 孩子回去。
你不能再让我一个人跟他玩了，我会累 死
的。"

"放心 吧，他明天就走了。"

Chapter 6
有钱人的孩子

想到 很快 就能拿 到钱了，我和老马都很开心。

"林哥，我们今天应该吃点儿好的。"

"对，我买 了很多肉 包子。你一定又累 又饿，多吃几个吧。"

"吃饭了！今天吃肉 包子。"老马 出去叫红猴。

"红猴，今天那么热，你怎么还穿 那么多衣服？"我一边洗手，一边说。"快去换衣服，一起来 吃包子 吧，很好吃的。"

看见那么多肉 包子，红猴 开心 地说："你们对我真好。"然后，他一下拿 了两

个包子。

"我不热，不想换 衣服。"红猴 吃得
很快。"真好吃！这是我吃过的最好吃的
包子。爸爸从来不 让我吃外面的东西。别
的孩子都可以自己买 好吃的，只有我不可

以。看他们吃的时候，我就很想哭，可是哭 也没有用……"

"你爸爸不在的时候，你也可以买 啊，他们不会知道的。"老马 说。

"我没钱，我爸爸从来不 给我钱。"

"你的朋友呢？你们买 包子 的时候，不会给你吃吗?"老马 问。

"我没有朋友，我爸爸不让我和别的孩子玩。他总是说，那些孩子的爸爸想要我们家的钱。"吃完包子，红猴 又喝了一口水，说:"他还说，等 我再大一点儿，就要送 我出国 上学，这里的朋友对我没有用。"

"林哥，我以为 有钱 人的孩子应该是很开心 的。可是，我看这个孩子好像 不怎

---

76 出国 (chūguó) *vo.* to leave the country

么开心。"老马 看着我，小声地说。

"我爸爸工作很忙，常常不在家，"红猴
有点难过 地说，"他只会跟我说，要好好
上学，多看书，这样才能出国。可是我一
点也不喜欢上学，我也不想出国。"

"红猴，别难过。"老马 又拿 了一个
包子 给他："我们给你买 好吃的，我们跟
你玩，好不好？"

"你们对我真好！"红猴 笑 了起来，"我
吃好了，不想吃了。我们来玩吧，你来做
坏人，我来抓 你。如果我抓 到了你，你就
要吃一只虫子。"孩子一边说，一边跑 过来
抓 老马。

"林哥，快帮 帮 我，我不要吃虫子……"

---

77 难过 (nánguò) *adj.* upset, sad　　78 帮 (bāng) *v.* to help

老马一边往山洞外面跑，一边大叫。"林哥，
快抓住他！"老马更大声了。

"红猴，你再这样，我们马上就送你
回家！"

"不要送我回家。"红猴有点儿怕

了，"我只是说说，不会真让老马 吃虫子的。"说完，他就一个人出去玩了。

"老马，下午我去树 下拿 钱。我回来以前，你跟红猴 玩，不能让他去别的地方。"

"林哥，你一定要快点回来！红猴 太可怕 了！我怕 我们还没拿 到钱，我就累死了。"

"放心 吧。"

Chapter 7
回信

下山以后，我先去了村子 里，路上一
个警察 也没看到。我不放心，又在村子 里
走了一会儿，也没看到有人在找孩子。

我在大树 的对面找了一个地方坐下
来。过了一会儿，一个女的在大树 下放 了
一个东西。

"没错，她就是高先生 家的人。"我开心
地想。

那个女的走了以后，我又等 了一会儿
才出来。树 下有一个大石头，我在石头 下
面找到了一个小包。

79 包 (bāo) *n.* bag, pack

　　"太好了！我们有钱 了！"我拿 起小包
就走。

　　我回到山洞 的时候，发现 老马 一个
人坐在地上。他看着我，可是不说话。

　　"老马，你怎么了？红猴 呢？他又打你

了吗?"

"林哥,红猴 不见了……"老马 小声地
说。

"怎么不见了? 我不是跟你说……好
吧, 没关系。"我拿 出那个小包,"你看, 我
已经拿 到钱了。"

"真的? 太好了!"老马 一下子 站了
起来,"有三千块钱吗? 快点打开 看看!"他
一边说, 一边打开 那个小包。可是, 包 里
没有钱, 只有信。

"钱呢? 为什么没有钱?"老马 大叫。

"天啊! 我以为 里面 放 的是三千块
钱……"我也没想到 会这样,"还是 先看看
信 上写了什么吧。"我一边说, 一边打开

高先生 的信。

两个不怕 死的人：

你们好。三千块钱太多了，我是不
会给的！你们最好马上 送 我儿子
回家，再给我五百块钱。如果你们
不这样做，我就告诉 警察。警察
一定会抓住 你们的！

高先生

"什么？！他不给我们钱，还让我们给
他五百块？！"我不相信 高先生 会问我们要
钱。"老马，快去找红猴！高先生 不给钱，
我们就不让他儿子回家！"

"林哥，对不起。我刚才 没有说真话。"

---

81 刚才 (gāngcái) *adv.* just now

82 真话 (zhēnhuà) *n.* the truth (lit.
"true speech")

"那你快说！发生 了什么事？！红猴

去哪儿了？"我生气 地对老马 大叫。

"我送 他回家了，我以为 你已经拿 到

钱了。林哥，红猴 太可怕 了。你刚走，他就要玩骑马，在我身上骑了半个多小时，还让我吃草！我不吃，他就打我。你知道他力气有多大吗？"老马好像快哭了。

"老马，我知道你很累……"

"林哥，这是我第一次吃草，你知不知道草有多难吃……我们怎么会抓一个这么可怕的孩子！"老马又生气又难过，"林哥，我真的是没有办法了，只能送他回家。我以为你已经拿到钱了。"

"老马，你真的送他回家了吗？"我看着外面问老马。

"林哥，我说的都是真话。我送他回去的路上，他还一直打我。你看，我的头，还有我身上，都红了！衣服也破了！"

"老马，你看，谁回来了？"

老马 觉得我的话有点奇怪，往 外面看了一下。红猴 回来了！他站在洞口，手里拿 着一块大石头，看起来 很不高兴。

"你这个坏人！我要让你看看谁最厉害！"红猴 大叫 着跑 了过来。

"啊……林哥，快帮帮我！"老马很怕，马上跑到我身后。

我抓住红猴的手："红猴，我们不是说好了吗？不能打老马，听话，快点放下石头。"

"我只是在跟他玩，不会真的打他。"红猴笑着说。

"红猴，老马刚才不是送你回家了吗？你怎么又回来了？"我问。

"我不想回家，我还想住在这儿，跟你们一起玩。"红猴放下了石头。

"如果你真的是这样想的，就要听我的话。老马太累了，今天要早点睡觉。你也早点睡，明天再玩，好不好？

"好吧，那我睡了。"红猴一边说，一

边放 自己的红衣服 在地上。"你今天去哪儿了？为什么你总是让老马 一个人跟我玩？你买 的肉 包子 真好吃，明天我还想吃。你们知不知道猴子是怎么叫的？老马，明天你一定要叫给我听……"红猴 说着说着就睡着 了。

Chapter 8
新的价格

第二天早上我起来 的时候，发现 我和老马 衣服 上面都有很多小洞。

"老马，我的衣服 也破 了……"

"林哥，你的衣服 比我好多了。你看我的衣服，这么破，还能穿 吗?"老马 不高兴 地说。

我穿 上衣服，走出山洞，看见红猴 正开心 地坐在树 上。

"你的衣服 怎么破 了？不过，衣服 上的洞很好看。"红猴 笑 着说。

"红猴，我知道是你做的。"我也对他笑了一下。

"你知道我是怎么做的吗?"红猴笑着问。

"你用的是火,对不对?"

"对,不过我用的火很小。如果火太大,你们今天就没衣服穿了。我对你们很好吧?"说完,红猴笑得更开心了。

"好了,快下来吃早饭吧。你昨天不是说还想吃我买的肉包子吗?"说完,我就进去拿包子了。

吃早饭的时候,老马大叫:"啊……林哥,包子里有石头!"

"包子里怎么会有……啊……石头,我也吃到了!"我放下包子,生气地看着红猴。

"真好玩！"红猴 开心 地说。吃完包子以后，他又到山洞 外面的树 上去玩了。

"林哥，高先生 不给钱，是不是不想要这个儿子了？"老马 问。

"高先生 一定会给钱的，他只是觉得我们的价格 有点高。"

"那我们就少要一点钱吧。林哥，两千块怎么样？"

"两千块是我们第一天想好的价格，后来如果不是因为你想多要一千，我们可能已经拿 到钱了。"我有点不高兴，"好了，不说了，现在就写信 吧。"

"真对不起，林哥。你来说，我来写。"

---

85 可能 (kěnéng) *aux.; n.* possibly; possibility

很快 信 就写好了。

"老马，快十点了。我现在下山去送信，很快 就回来。"

我进村子 的时候，看见一些人正在说话。我走近了一点，想听听他们在说什么。

"已经两三天了，不知道是不是坏人进了村子，抓 走了孩子？"

"也有可能 是自己跑 出去玩，找不到回家的路了。谁知道呢！"

"这个孩子在村子 里只会做坏事，如果真的是坏人抓 走的，我看是好事。"一个人说，"有一次，这孩子来我家拿 我儿子的东西玩，玩坏了以后，也不说'对不起'。我儿子问他的时候，他还打我儿子！"这个人很生气，"听我儿子说，他还常常在别的孩子的衣服 上写字，老师也没办法 管 他。"

这个人刚刚说完，一个人又说："我看是高先生 自己不会管 孩子。有一次，我儿子在吃东西，这孩子也想吃。我儿子没

给他，他就拿 石头 打我儿子的头！我去
找高先生 的时候，你们知道他跟我说什
么吗?"他听起来 更生气 了，"高先生 什么
都没说，只给了我们两百块钱，就让我们
走！"

"如果不是因为他太小，警察 早就来抓
他了！"一个老人说，"我听说，前几天村子
里来了几个坏人，孩子是他们抓 走的。他
们让高先生 给三千块钱，如果高先生 不
给，就见不到他儿子了。"

"三千块？这些人真可笑。高先生 一
定不会给那么多钱的。你们相不相信?"

"我看，一半的钱他也不会给。"

听到人们这样说，我才发现 我们想错

了。孩子那么难管，可能 高先生 也不想那么快让他回家。高先生 在信 里说，三千块太多了。那对他来说，两千块这个价格 会不会还是 太高了？我想了一下，还是 先回去吧，不去送 信 了。

— Chapter 9 —
最后的价格

"信送到了吗？"老马看我回来得这么早，很开心。

"我进了村子，但是没去送信。"我喝了一口水，说："老马，这孩子在村子里做了太多坏事，村子里的大人和孩子都不喜欢他。我们抓了他，他们都很高兴。还有，他们都觉得高先生不会给那么多钱。"

"林哥，你是说，两千块还是太多了？"老马小声问。"如果再少一点呢？一千块，你觉得他会给吗？"

"一千块有点少，不过，"我想了一下，"能拿到钱就好。老马，这次我们一定

要拿 到钱。明天就送 红猴 回家，问高先生要钱。一千块是我们最后的价格，不能再少了。"

"林哥，如果红猴 发现 我们要送 他回家，一定会打死我的。"老马 很怕。

"别怕，我有办法，他不会发现 的。今天晚上，等 红猴 睡着 了，我们就开车 带他进村子。我们都睡在车里，在高先生 家门口等 一个晚上。"

"这个办法 好。晚上人们都睡了，应该不会有人看到我们。"老马 听起来 很开心。

"再说，也不可能 有警察。"我喝了一口水，"明天早上，我会早点起来，去高先生家问他要钱。你在车里看着红猴。"

"可是，如果红猴 起来 了怎么办？"
4

"那你就跟他在车上玩一会儿。再说，

高先生 应该很快 就会给钱，我拿 到钱，
30   18

马上 放 他回家。"
66 11

"林哥，我怕 红猴 ……他起来 以后一
38   4

定会打我的……"

"老马，我知道你很累……"

"不只是累！你看我身上，都是红的，
都是他打的。还有我的衣服，都是洞！"
老马很生气，可是又不能太大声。

"老马，这是最后一次去要钱。放心
吧！我们一定会拿到这一千块钱的！"

老马没说话，他真的怕明天红猴会
打他，但是也只能听我的话。

晚上，我们给红猴做了一些好吃的。
吃完以后，红猴很开心："你们对我真好，
从来没有人对我这么好。我真喜欢跟你们
玩。"然后，他对老马说："老马，你知不知
道猴子是怎么叫的？"

87 从来没 (cónglái méi) *phrase* have
never

"不知道。"

"我觉得它们是这样叫的，你听我叫，然后跟我学。"说完，红猴 就大声 叫了起来。我也不知道猴子是怎么叫的，只是觉得他叫得很难听。

"太难了，我不会。"老马 说。

"一点也不难，你试试。"红猴 又叫了一声。

"红猴，我们今天都很累，想早点睡觉，明天老马 再跟你玩吧。"我一边说，一边在地上放 几件 很大的衣服。

"每次都是老马 跟我玩，明天你也要跟我们一起玩。"红猴 看着我说。

---

88 难听 (nántīng) *adj.* terrible-sounding

89 试试 (shìshi) *phrase* to give it a try

"好，没问题。快睡吧。"我笑着说。

晚上十二点的时候，红猴已经睡着了，我让老马去开车。红猴睡在车的后面，我们坐在前面。

上车以后，我看了一下红猴，小声

说：“路上一定要小心，要开慢一点。还有，我们在车里要少说话，说话的时候要小声点。”

“好，我知道了。”老马 小声地说。

下山的路上一个人也没有，我们的车慢慢地 进了村子。

“林哥，高先生 家到了。”

“好，现在才一点，我们也睡吧。”

“别忘了明天早点起来。”说完，老马很快 就睡着 了。

— Chapter 10 —
再见

　　第二天早上六点半，我就起来了。红猴和老马都还在睡觉。我下了车，在高先生家门口等着。七点多的时候，高先生走了出来。

　　"你好，高先生。我是那个给你写信的人，你儿子一直在我们这儿。我们送他回来了。"

　　"我就知道你会送他回来。"高先生笑着说。

　　"你一定很想快点见到你儿子，只要你给一千块，我们马上就放他回家。"

　　"我给你们一千块？我看你们还是没

明白我的信 的意思。"高先生 又笑 了,"你
们真的想要我儿子吗?"

这时候,老马 大叫 着从车上跑 下
来:"啊……林哥,快帮 帮 我……"

"你们不是说不会送 我回家的吗?"

红猴 生气 地大叫。

"儿子，"高先生 看看红猴，又看看老马，"这个人身上 那么红，是不是你打的？还有，他衣服 上怎么有那么多洞？你是不是又玩火 了？"

"我只是在跟他玩。"红猴 刚说完，又对老马 大叫："我要打死你！"

"啊……别打了……林哥，我们快点走吧，一千块钱我们不要了……"老马 好像真的累 坏了，他现在只想走。

"我要让你知道红猴 的厉害！"红猴一下子 骑 到了老马 身上，不知道他从哪儿拿 出来一只虫子，放 进了老马 的衣服里。

"啊……"老马 最怕 虫子 了，"林哥，我不行了，快点让人带 走这个孩子……"

"放心 吧，我会带 走我儿子的。"高先生说，"你们带 我儿子玩了几天，是在帮 我，我应该谢谢你们。不过，你们还是 要给五百块钱。"

"不行，我们为这个孩子已经花了一些钱，现在怎么能给他钱呢？"我生气 地想，然后说："高先生，我们不想跟你做这个生意 了。我们现在就放 你儿子回家，但是，我们不可能 给你五百块钱。"

"你看看你的朋友吧，他身上 都是红的，衣服 也破 了。问问他，是不是还想让红猴 一直骑 在身上？"高先生 笑 了一下，"我看他快要累 死了。"

"林哥，快点给他钱吧……"老马 好像快没力气 了。

看我一直不说话，高先生 问红猴："儿子，这几天你跟他们在一起是不是玩得很开心？"

红猴 看着高先生，用力 点了点头。

"你想不想跟他们再多玩几天？"高先生 问。

"当然想！"红猴 很开心，大声 说。"爸爸，让我跟他们一起走吧。"

听到红猴 这么说，我真的不知道怎么办了。

"林哥，我不要再跟这个孩子玩了，一天也不要……"老马 看着我，好像 快哭 了。

我没办法，只能给高先生 五百块。
<u>9</u>

高先生 马上 过去抓住 了红猴，说："儿子，
<u>66</u>　　　<u>61</u>

他们好像 累 坏了，下次吧。"
<u>52</u>　<u>44</u>

"不要抓 我！我不要回家！"红猴 对
<u>10</u>

高先生 大叫。"我要跟老马 一起玩！"
<u>35</u>

老马 慢慢站了起来，他还在找刚才红猴 放 在他衣服 里的虫子。

"你们现在知道红猴 有多厉害 了吧?"高先生 笑 着说，"你们快跑 吧！我不能一直抓 着他。如果你们还不快跑，他一定会找到你们的。"

高先生 刚说 完，老马 就跑 了。我从来没 见过老马 跑 得那么快。

Key Words 关键词 (Guānjiàncí)

1. 村子 (cūnzi) *n.* village, town
2. 生意 (shēngyì) *n.* business
3. 买 (mǎi) *v.* to buy
4. 起来 (qǐlai) *v.* to get up
5. 开心 (kāixīn) *adj.* happy
6. 有钱 (yǒuqián) *adj.* rich; to have money
7. 笑 (xiào) *v.* to laugh, to smile
8. 想到 (xiǎngdào) *vc.* to think of
9. 办法 (bànfǎ) *n.* way of doing
10. 抓 (zhuā) *v.* to grab
11. 放 (fàng) *v.* to put, to release
12. 警察 (jǐngchá) *n.* police
13. 跑 (pǎo) *v.* to run
14. 山洞 (shāndòng) *n.* cave (in the mountains)
15. 带 (dài) *v.* to carry
16. 价格 (jiàgé) *n.* price
17. 力气 (lìqi) *n.* strength
18. 拿 (ná) *v.* to pick up
19. 石头 (shítou) *n.* stone
20. 以为 (yǐwéi) *v.* to (mistakenly) think that
21. 从来不 (cónglái bù) *phrase* never
22. 上学 (shàngxué) *vo.* to go to school
23. 发现 (fāxiàn) *v.* to discover
24. 还是 (háishi) *conj.; adv.* still; had better
25. 听话 (tīnghuà) *vo.* to be obedient, to listen
26. 管 (guǎn) *v.* to manage, to handle
27. 等 (děng) *v.* to wait
28. 出门 (chūmén) *vo.* to go out the door
29. 信 (xìn) *n.* letter
30. 很快 (hěn kuài) *phrase* quickly, soon

31. 开车 (kāichē) *vo.* to drive (a car)

32. 高兴 (gāoxìng) *adj.* happy

33. 件 (jiàn) *mw.* [measure word for clothing, incidents]

34. 哭 (kū) *v.* to cry

35. 大叫 (dàjiào) *v.* to cry out loudly

36. 大声 (dàshēng) *adv.* loudly

37. 打开 (dǎkāi) *vc.* to open

38. 怕 (pà) *v.* to fear

39. 用力 (yònglì) *vo.* to use force

40. 厉害 (lìhai) *adj.* impressive

41. 放心 (fàngxīn) *v.* to relax

42. 睡觉 (shuìjiào) *vo.* to sleep

43. 衣服 (yīfu) *n.* clothing

44. 累 (lèi) *adj.* tired

45. 睡着 (shuìzháo) *vc.* to fall asleep

46. 穿 (chuān) *v.* to put on, to wear

47. 小心 (xiǎoxīn) *v.* to be careful

48. 洞口 (dòngkǒu) *n.* mouth of a cave

49. 奇怪 (qíguài) *adj.* strange

50. 树 (shù) *n.* tree

51. 往 (wǎng) *cov.* toward

52. 好像 (hǎoxiàng) *adv.* it seems (that)

53. 换 (huàn) *v.* to change

54. 像 (xiàng) *v.* to resemble

55. 生气 (shēngqì) *vo.* to get angry

56. 虫子 (chóngzi) *n.* bug, insect, worm

57. 好玩 (hǎowán) *adj.* fun, amusing

58. 一下子 (yīxiàzi) *adv.* all at once

59. 骑 (qí) *v.* to ride on

60. 身上 (shēnshang) *n.* on one's body

61. 抓住 (zhuāzhù) *vc.* to grab hold of

62. 送 (sòng) *v.* to send, to deliver, to take (someone to a place)

63. 相信 (xiāngxìn) *v.* to believe

64. 告诉 (gàosu) *v.* to tell

65. 没想到 (méi xiǎngdào) *phrase* to never have imagined

66. 马上 (mǎshàng) *adv.* right away

67. 放下 (fàngxia) *vc.* to put down

68. 可怕 (kěpà) *adj.* scary

69. 里面 (lǐmiàn) *n.* inside

70. 肉 (ròu) *n.* meat

71. 包子 (bāozi) *n.* steamed bun

72. 卖 (mài) *v.* to sell

73. 不用 (bùyòng) *phrase* no need

74. 草 (cǎo) *n.* grass

75. 破 (pò) *adj.* worn out, beat-up

76. 出国 (chūguó) *vo.* to leave the country

77. 难过 (nánguò) *adj.* upset, sad

78. 帮 (bāng) *v.* to help

79. 包 (bāo) *n.* bag, pack

80. 关系 (guānxi) *n.* relationship

81. 刚才 (gāngcái) *adv.* just now

82. 真话 (zhēnhuà) *n.* the truth (lit. "true speech")

83. 发生 (fāshēng) *v.* to happen

84. 火 (huǒ) *n.* fire

85. 可能 (kěnéng) *aux.; n.* possibly; possibility

86. 可笑 (kěxiào) *adj.* laughable

87. 从来没 (cónglái méi) *phrase* have never

88. 难听 (nántīng) *adj.* terrible-sounding

89. 试试 (shìshi) *phrase* to give it a try

90. 慢慢地 (mànmàn de) *adv.* slowly

Part of Speech Key

adj. Adjective

adv. Adverb

aux. Auxiliary Verb

conj. Conjunction

cov. Coverb

mw. Measure word

n. Noun

on. Onomatopoeia

part. Particle

prep. Preposition

pn. Proper noun

tn. Time Noun

v. Verb

vc. Verb plus complement

vo. Verb plus object

Discussion Questions
讨论问题 (Tǎolùn Wèntí)

Chapter 1 一个生意

1. 老马和林哥为什么要抓孩子？

2. 高先生是谁？为什么村子里的人都不喜欢他儿子？

3. 你觉得父母可以打孩子吗？为什么？

4. 你小时候做过什么坏事吗？请说一说。

Chapter 2 抓人

1. 去抓孩子以前，老马和林哥想了什么办法让孩子跟他们走？

2. 第一次，孩子不听他们的话，所以林哥又想了什么办法？如果你是林哥，你会想什么办法？

3. 孩子为什么很喜欢山里，也不想回家？

4. 你小时候，有没有在外面跟不认识的人一起住过？你会怕吗？请说一说。

Chapter 3 红猴来了

1. 孩子和红猴是什么关系？

2. 红猴为什么要打老马？

3. 为什么老马不想让红猴找到他的衣服？

4. 如果坏人抓住了你，你会想什么办法回家？

5. 如果你是林哥和老马，你会怎么写这个信？

Chapter 4 写信

1. 你觉得林哥怕红猴吗？如果让你跟这样的孩子在一起住几天，你会怎么办？

2. 为什么老马要让高先生多给一千块？

3. 孩子让老马跟他一起玩的时候，老马为什么不开心？

4. 如果让你跟一个不听话的孩子在一起，你会想什么办法让他听话？

Chapter 5 送信

1. 送完信以后，林哥做了什么？
2. 在高先生家工作的人也知道孩子不见了，她怎么看这件事？
3. 你觉得高先生正在找孩子吗？为什么？
4. 林哥回来的时候，红猴在做什么？
5. 如果你认识的一个人总是对你很不好，可是你每天都会见到他，你会怎么办？

Chapter 6 有钱人的孩子

1. 为什么高先生不让自己的孩子跟别的孩子玩？
2. 为什么高先生很有钱，可是他儿子一点也不开心？
3. 你的父母会给你钱吗？你会怎么花这些钱？
4. 在中国，很多有钱人想送孩子出国，在你的国家呢？

Chapter 7 回信

1. 下山以后，林哥为什么要先去村子里看看？
2. 高先生的回信里有钱吗？林哥他们看到信以后怎么想？
3. 你觉得林哥他们会给五百块钱吗？为什么？
4. 老马为什么要送孩子回去？

Chapter 8 新的价格

1. 说一说林哥的第二个信是怎么写的。
2. 村子里的人为什么不喜欢这个孩子？你觉得他是坏孩子吗？为什么？
3. 如果你是林哥，你还会去送第二个信吗？为什么？

Chapter 9 最后的价格

1. 最后的价格是多少？你觉得高先生这次会给钱吗？为什么？
2. 他们为什么要很晚的时候开车去村子里？
3. 如果孩子发现了他们带他回家了，你觉得会发生什么？

Chapter 10 再见

1. 高先生一直没告诉警察，也没让警察来抓他们，你觉得这是为什么？

2. 如果你是高先生，你会马上让警察来抓林哥和老马吗？为什么？

3. 林哥为什么要给高先生五百块钱？如果你是林哥，你会怎么做？为什么？

4. 你觉得这个故事好玩吗？为什么？

Appendix A:
Character Comparison Reference

This appendix is designed to help Chinese teachers and learners use the Mandarin Companion graded readers as a companion to the most popular university textbooks and the HSK word lists.

The tables below compare the characters and vocabulary used in other study materials with those found in this Mandarin Companion graded reader. The tables below will display the exact characters and vocabulary used in this book and not covered by these sources. A learner who has studied these textbooks will likely find it easier to read this graded reader by focusing on these characters and words.

Integrated Chinese Level 1, Part 1-2 (3rd Ed.)

Words and characters in this story not covered by these textbooks:

Character	Pinyin	Word(s)	Pinyin
猴	hóu	红猴 猴子	Hóng Hóu hóuzi
林	lín	林哥	Lín Gē
村	cūn	村子	cūnzi
抓	zhuā	抓 抓住	zhuā zhuāzhù
山	shān	山 山洞	shān shāndòng
声	shēng	一声 大声 小声	yī shēng dàshēng xiǎoshēng
洞	dòng	山洞 洞口 洞	shāndòng dòngkǒu dòng
树	shù	树	shù
石	shí	石头	shítou

Character	Pinyin	Word(s)	Pinyin
厉	lì	厉害	lìhai
害	hài	厉害	lìhai
管	guǎn	管	guǎn
虫	chóng	虫子	chóngzi
价	jià	价格	jiàgé
格	gé	价格	jiàgé
警	jǐng	警察	jǐngchá
察	chá	警察	jǐngchá
骑	qí	骑 骑马	qí qímǎ
破	pò	破	pò
门	mén	出门 门口 车门 大门	chūmén ménkǒu chēmén dàmén
草	cǎo	草	cǎo
总	zǒng	总是	zǒngshì
相	xiāng	相信	xiāngxìn
刀	dāo	刀	dāo
火	huǒ	火	huǒ
怪	guài	奇怪	qíguài
奇	qí	奇怪	qíguài
杀	shā	杀死	shāsǐ

New Practical Chinese Reader, Books 1-2 (1st Ed.)

Words and characters in this story not covered by these textbooks:

Character	Pinyin	Word(s)	Pinyin
猴	hóu	红猴 猴子	Hóng Hóu hóuzi

Character	Pinyin	Word(s)	Pinyin
洞	dòng	山洞 洞口 洞	shāndòng dòngkǒu dòng
厉	lì	厉害	lìhai
虫	chóng	虫子	chóngzi
直	zhí	一直	yīzhí
价	jià	价格	jiàgé
破	pò	破	pò
草	cǎo	草	cǎo
更	gèng	更	gèng
杀	shā	杀死	shāsǐ
奇	qí	奇怪	qíguài
怪	guài	奇怪	qíguài
父	fù	父母	fùmǔ
母	mǔ	父母	fùmǔ
近	jìn	近	jìn

Hanyu Shuiping Kaoshi (HSK) Levels 1-3

Words and characters in this story not covered by these levels:

Character	Pinyin	Word(s)	Pinyin
猴	hóu	红猴 猴子	Hóng Hóu hóuzi
林	lín	林哥	Lín Gē
村	cūn	村子	cūnzi
抓	zhuā	抓 抓住	zhuā zhuāzhù
洞	dòng	山洞 洞口 洞	shāndòng dòngkǒu dòng

Character	Pinyin	Word(s)	Pinyin
石	shí	石头	shítou
厉	lì	厉害	lìhai
管	guǎn	管	guǎn
死	sǐ	杀死	shāsǐ
虫	chóng	虫子	chóngzi
价	jià	价格	jiàgé
格	gé	价格	jiàgé
警	jǐng	警察	jǐngchá
察	chá	警察	jǐngchá
破	pò	破	pò
刀	dāo	刀	dāo
杀	shā	杀死	shāsǐ
父	fù	父母	fùmǔ
母	mǔ	父母	fùmǔ

Appendix B: Grammar Point Index

For learners new to reading Chinese, an understanding of grammar points can be extremely helpful for learners and teachers. The following is a list of the most challenging grammar points used in this graded reader.

These grammar points correspond to the Common European Framework of Reference for Languages (CEFR) level A2 or above. The full list with explanations and examples of each grammar point can be found on the Chinese Grammar Wiki, the definitive source of information on Chinese grammar online.

CHAPTER 1	
Special verbs with "hen"	很 + Verb
Actions in a row	(Verb Phrase 1) + (Verb Phrase 2)
Two words for "but"	……，可是 / 但是……
Expressing "only" with "zhi"	只 + Verb
Indicating a number in excess	Number + 多
Using "dui" with verbs	对 + Noun……
Auxiliary verb "yao" and its multiple meanings	要 + Noun / 要 + Verb
Expressing "and also" with "hai"	还 + Verb
Modifying nouns with phrase + "de"	Phrase + 的 + Noun
Adjectives with "name" and "zheme"	那么 / 这么 + Adj.
Appearance with "kanqilai"	看起来……
Indicating location with "zai" before verbs	Subj. + 在 + Place + Verb
Aspect particle "zhe"	Verb + 着
Expressing "not very" with "bu tai"	不太 + Adj.
Expressing "every" with "mei"	每 + Measure Word (+ Noun)
Expressing "when" with "de shihou"	……的时候
Emphasizing quantity with "dou"	大家 / 很多人 + 都……

Expressing "together" with "yiqi"	一起 + Verb
Modifying nouns with adjective + "de"	Adj. + 的 + Noun
Expressing completion with "le"	Subj. + Verb + 了 + Obj.
Causative verbs	Noun 1 + 让 / 叫 / 请 + Noun 2……
Expressing earliness with "jiu"	Subj. + Time Word + 就 + Verb + 了
Expressing "if…, then…" with "ruguo…, jiu…"	如果……，就……
Expressing "will" with "hui"	会 + Verb
Verbs that take double objects	Subj. + Verb + Indirect Obj. + Direct Obj.
Turning adjectives into adverbs	Adj. + 地 + Verb
Structural particle "de"	的 / 得 / 地
Expressing "some" with "yixie"	一些 + Noun
Special cases of "zai" following verbs	Verb + 在 + Place
Tricky uses of "dao"	Verb + 到
Superlative "zui"	最 + Adj.
Phrases using "laishuo"	……来说
Expressing "in addition" with "zaishuo"	再说……
Using "gen" to mean "with"	跟…… + Verb
Cause and effect with "yinwei" and "suoyi"	因为……所以……
Expressing "always" with "zongshi"	总是 + Verb
Expressing "all along" with "yizhi"	Subj. + 一直 + Predicate
Expressing "mistakenly think that" with "yiwei"	以为……
Expressing "never" with "conglai"	从来 + 不 / 没 (有) + Verb
Continuation with "hai"	还在 + Verb / Adj.
Using "hao" to mean "easy"	好 + Verb

A softer "but" with "buguo"	⋯⋯，不过 ⋯⋯
Verbing briefly with "yixia"	Verb + 一下
After a specific time with "yihou"	Time / Verb + 以后
Verbs preceded by "gei"	Subj. + 给 + Target + Verb + Obj.
Sequencing with "xian" and "zai"	先 ⋯⋯ 再 ⋯⋯
Expressing "when" with "dengdao"	等 (到) + ⋯⋯，Subj. + 再 / 就 / 才 ⋯⋯

CHAPTER 2

Result complements	Verb + 好
Using "dao" to mean "to go to"	到 + Place
Expressing "already" with "yijing"	已经 ⋯⋯ 了
Using "de" (modal particle)	⋯⋯ 的
Simultaneous tasks with "yibian"	一边 + Verb 1，一边 + Verb 2
Measure words for verbs	Verb + Number + Measure Word
Expressing "again" in the past with "you"	又 + Verb
Result complements "-dao" and "-jian"	Verb + 到 / 见
Expressing "just" with "gang"	Subj. + 刚 + Verb
Doing something more with "duo"	多 + Verb
Softening speech with "ba"	⋯⋯ 吧
Expressing "again" in the future with "zai"	再 + Verb
Direction complement	Verb (+ Direction) + 来 / 去
Questions with "le ma"	Verb + 了 + 吗?
Name-calling with "zhege"	Noun + 这个 + Category
Expressing "really" with "zhen"	真 + Adj.
Negative commands with "bie"	别 + Verb
Expressing "much more" in comparisons	Noun 1 + 比 + Noun 2 + Adj. + 多 了 / 得多
Intensifying with "duo"	Subj. + 多 + Adj.

CHAPTER 5

Expressing "even more" with "geng"	更 + Adj.
Expressing "every" with question words	谁 / 哪里 + 都
Inability with "mei banfa"	没办法 + Verb
Asking why with "zenme"	怎么······?
Expressing lateness with "cai"	Subj. + Time + 才 + Verb-Obj.
Expressing experiences with "guo"	Verb + 过

CHAPTER 6

Expressing "should" with "yinggai"	应该 / 该 + Verb
Expressing "both A and B" with "you"	又······又······
Expressing "now" with "le"	······了
Expressing "before" in general with "yiqian"	以前，······
Expressing "not very" with "bu zenme"	不怎么 + Adj.
Expressing "not anymore" with "le"	不 / 没 (有) + Verb Phrase + 了

CHAPTER 7

Change of state with "le"	······了
Expressing "had better" with "zui-hao"	Subj. + 最好 + Verb Phrase
Expressing "just now" with "gangcai"	刚才 + Verb
Using "zhe" when "verbing away"	Verb + 着 + Verb + 着

CHAPTER 8

Expressing location with "zai... shang / xia / li"	在 + Place + 上 / 下 / 里 / 旁边
Doing something less with "shao"	少 + Verb
Advanced yes-no questions with "ma"	······吗?
Expressing "everything" with "shenme dou"	什么 + 都 / 也······

CHAPTER 9

Expressing "not even one"	一 + Measure Word + (Noun) + 也 / 都 + Verb
Turning adjectives into adverbs	Adj. + 地 + Verb

CHAPTER 10

Expressing "as long as" with "zhiyao"	只要······，就······
Expressing "for" with "wei"	为 + Noun······

Other Stories from Mandarin Companion

Level 1 Readers: 300 Characters

The Secret Garden 《秘密花园》
by Frances Hodgson Burnett

After an epidemic leaves her an orphan, Li Ye is sent off to live with her reclusive uncle in his sprawling estate in Nanjing. She learns of a secret garden where no one has set foot in ten years. With the help of new friends, she brings the garden back to life and learns the healing power of friendship and love.

The Sixty Year Dream 《六十年的梦》
based on Rip Van Winkle by Washington Irving

Zhou Xuefa (Rip Van Winkle) is well loved by everyone in his town, except his nagging wife. One day after a bad scolding from his wife, he goes for a walk into the mountains and meets a mysterious old man. After drinking some wine offered by the old man, Zhou Xuefa falls into a deep sleep. He awakes to a time very different than what he once knew.

The Monkey's Paw 《猴爪》
by W. W. Jacobs

Mr. and Mrs. Zhang live with their grown son. One day an old friend comes to visit and tells of a monkey's paw that has magical powers to grant three wishes to the holder. Against his better judgment, he reluctantly gives the monkey paw to the Zhang family, with a warning that the wishes come with a great price for trying to change fate.

The Country of the Blind 《盲人国》
by H. G. Wells

Chen Fangyuan finds himself trapped in a valley with a people for whom a disease has eliminated their vision and no longer have a concept of sight. His insistence that he can see causes the entire community to think he is crazy. Then one day the village doctors propose a disturbing cure for his insanity.

Sherlock Holmes and the Case of the Curly-Haired Company 《卷发公司的案子》
based on The Red Headed League by Sir Arthur Conan Doyle

Mr. Xie was recently hired by the Curly Haired Company to copy articles from a book. He was selected from hundreds of applicants because of his very curly hair. When the company unexpectedly closes, Mr. Xie visits Gao Ming (Sherlock Holmes) with his strange story. Gao Ming is certain something is not right, but will he solve the mystery in time?

The Prince and the Pauper 《王子和穷孩子》
by Mark Twain

During a chance encounter, two nearly identical boys, one a poor beggar and the other a prince, exchange places. Both children soon discover that neither life is as carefree as they expected.

Emma 《安末》
by Jane Austen

Clever, rich, and single, the beautiful An Mo (Emma Woodhouse) is focused on her career as fashion designer in the glamor of 21st-century Shanghai. She sees no need for romance in her life, but when she tries to find a boyfriend for her new friend Fangfang (Harriet), her carefully laid plans being to unravel. As she ignores the warnings of her good friend Shi Wenzheng (Mr. Knightley), her decisions bring consequences that she never expected. With its witty and charming characters, Emma is often seen as Jane Austen's most flawless work.

Level 2 Readers: 450 Characters

Great Expectations: Part 1 《美好的前途（上）》
by Charles Dickens

In Part 1, Xiaomao is raised by his short-tempered older sister and her husband outside of Shanghai. After meeting the beautiful Bingbing (Estella), Xiaomao dreams of leaving his life of poverty behind. His prospects for the future are bleak, until one day a mysterious benefactor gives Xiaomao the opportunity of a lifetime.

Great Expectations: Part 2 《美好的前途（下）》
by Charles Dickens

In Part 2, Xiaomao (Pip) leaves his life of poverty behind to seek his fortunes in Shanghai and win the heart of the beautiful yet cold-hearted Bingbing (Estella). Xiaomao's world is turned upside down when his mysterious benefactor is revealed and his deepest secrets are brought into the light of day.

Journey to the Center of the Earth 《地心游记》
by Jules Verne

Join Professor Luo and his niece Xiaojing in their daring quest down the mouth of a volcano to reach the center of the earth. Guided by a mysterious passage on an ancient parchment and accompanied by their faithful guide Lao Xu, the three explorers encounter subterranean phenomena, prehistoric animals, and vast underground seas.

Mandarin Companion is producing a growing library of graded readers for Chinese language learners.

Visit our website for the newest books available:

www.MandarinCompanion.com

CPSIA information can be obtained
at www.ICGtesting.com
Printed in the USA
BVHW092148270121
598864BV00003B/119